INSECTS

Written by David Drew • Illustrated by Marilyn Pride

Collins Educational
An imprint of HarperCollins*Publishers*

CONTENTS

ANTS

All ants are insects.

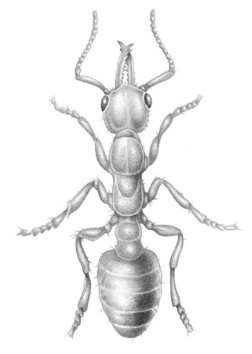

- ■ head
- □ thorax
- □ abdomen
- ■ legs

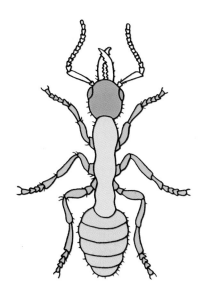

BEES

All bees are insects.

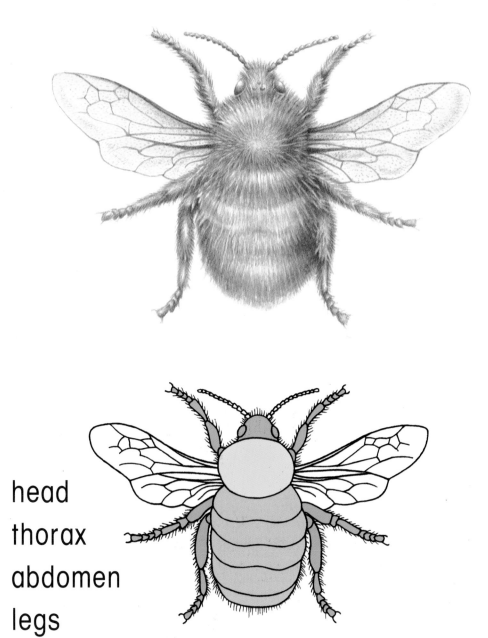

- ■ head
- □ thorax
- ▨ abdomen
- ▨ legs

All flies are insects.

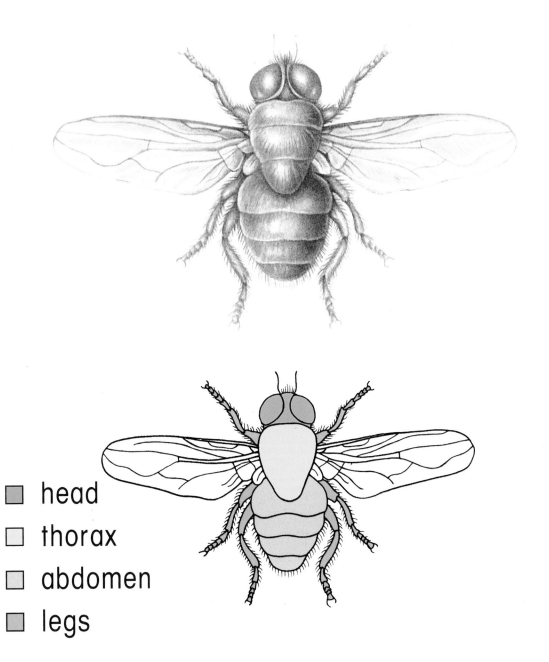

☐ head
☐ thorax
☐ abdomen
☐ legs

BEETLES

All beetles are insects.

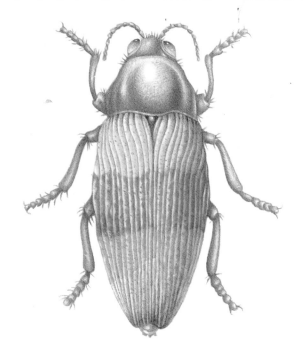

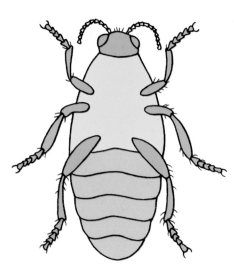

- 🟦 head
- ⬜ thorax
- 🟩 abdomen
- 🟪 legs

All dragonflies are insects.

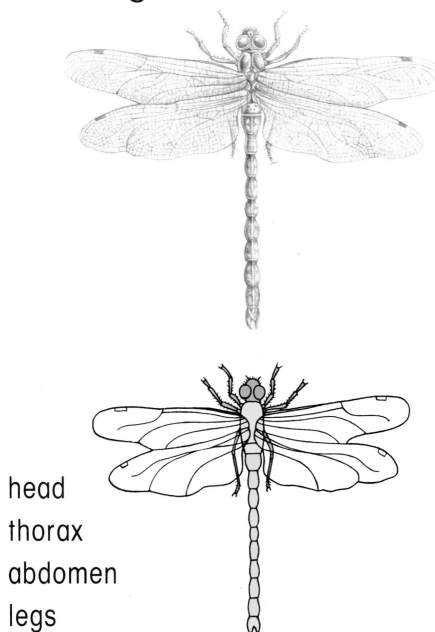

■ head

☐ thorax

☐ abdomen

■ legs

All insects have:

◻ a head,

◻ a thorax,

◻ an abdomen

◻ and 6 legs.